T0194899

The *Perfect* Tree for Mrs. B.

Deborah Wagner-Brenneman

Illustrated by: Melinda Bishoff

Copyright © 2018 Deborah Wagner-Brenneman.

All rights reserved. No part of this book may be used or reproduced by any means, graphic, electronic, or mechanical, including photocopying, recording, taping or by any information storage retrieval system without the written permission of the author except in the case of brief quotations embodied in critical articles and reviews.

Scripture taken from the New King James Version®. Copyright © 1982 by Thomas Nelson. Used by permission. All rights reserved.

WestBow Press books may be ordered through booksellers or by contacting:

WestBow Press
A Division of Thomas Nelson & Zondervan
1663 Liberty Drive
Bloomington, IN 47403
www.westbowpress.com
1 (866) 928-1240

Because of the dynamic nature of the Internet, any web addresses or links contained in this book may have changed since publication and may no longer be valid. The views expressed in this work are solely those of the author and do not necessarily reflect the views of the publisher, and the publisher hereby disclaims any responsibility for them.

Any people depicted in stock imagery provided by Getty Images are models, and such images are being used for illustrative purposes only.
Certain stock imagery © Getty Images.

ISBN: 978-1-9736-3710-3 (sc)
ISBN: 978-1-9736-3711-0 (e)

Library of Congress Control Number: 2018909664

Print information available on the last page.

WestBow Press rev. date: 08/21/2018

WESTBOW
P R E S S®
A DIVISION OF THOMAS NELSON
& ZONDERVAN

Dedication

Deborah –

To my loving husband, Terry. I thank you for your endless support and sharing your life with me.

To my loyal and dear friend, Laura. Thanks for all of the memories.

Melinda –

To my son, Mason…you are precious in my sight.

I will praise You, for I am fearfully and wonderfully made; Marvelous are Your works, And that my soul knows very well.

—Psalm 139:14 (NKJV)

Every November, Mrs. B. would travel to the Christmas tree farm that was beside the school where she taught. She wouldn't go alone; She would take her twenty Pre-K students and her beloved assistant, Mrs. Bolden.

Down the road, they passed the big red barn. They would travel hand in hand with a partner and a purpose. They would find the perfect tree for Mrs. B.

The perfect tree that would be beautiful with decorations of red and green ornaments, white lights, and multi-colored tinsel that would glisten throughout the home of Mrs. B.

The trees stood in rows as though they knew they were on display for the main event, Christmas. Beautifully poised with confidence that no one could take away, each tree would sway in the breeze and whisper, "Choose me, choose me."

The children would begin to encircle the trees and giggle as the branches brushed against their faces or tripped them, and they rolled onto the ground beneath the trees.

As they played and danced around the trees, Mrs. B. would say to the children, "Find me a tree. The most beautiful tree." Find the perfect tree for Mrs. B.

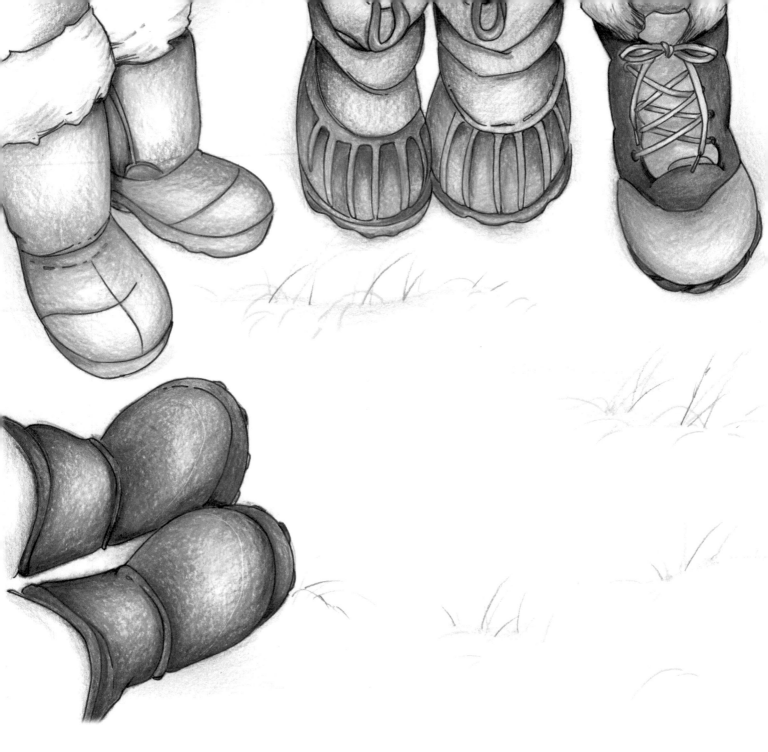

As the children looked at the trees, they began to ask questions about the appearance of the trees. They asked, "Mrs. B, do you want this tree?

"Hmm, no, too short," she replied.

"This tree?" they prompted.

"Too fat, too tall, too skinny, dead branches, or not enough branches," Mrs. B. would reply. We must find the perfect tree for Mrs. B.

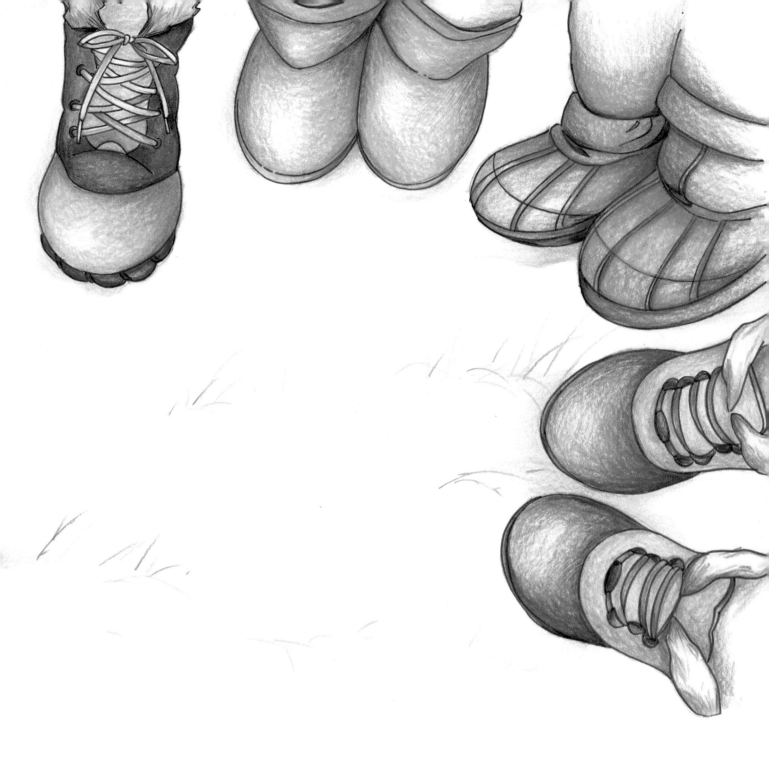

The children began to break away from the large group and visit other areas with their partners on the tree farm.

The trees were different, yet the same. All the trees needed sunshine. All the trees needed water. All the trees were green and all the trees had a purpose.

The trees were on a tree farm and they would stand proudly until someone would come, dig them up, put them in a bucket of soil, and place them in their home for a week or two to celebrate Christmas.

And then, the tree would be replanted at the home of the owner or
donated to a school or park to beautify it.

"This is it, this is it! Come here, Mrs. B!"

There stood Colton and Eli at the perfect tree.

The tree was a white pine. It stood 8 feet tall, and we knew it was a white pine because the needles were in a bundle of five. And we learned a little trick; the word white has five letters and the needles were in clusters of five. Therefore, we knew how to identify a white pine tree. But, Mrs. B. said the tree was too tall and wouldn't fit in the room she was going to place the tree in at her home.

So, the children traveled down another row and Mrs. B. heard one little boy yelling, "Over here, over here! It is perfect, Mrs. B. It is perfect!" The children ran to the spot and there stood a short, chubby tree with a little bend in the middle that made it slightly imperfect. It was spruce; it had a bluish-green tint and wasn't the typical green that Mrs. B. was used to.

"Let's keep searching," said Mrs. B. "There has to be the perfect tree."

At this point, the students became marching soldiers. They started the mission of perfection on a new side of the tree farm. They began looking at all sides of the trees, getting under the tree and looking up for bare, open spots. They began standing back and looking for bends in the middle or a broken branch or a bushy top or too much pine pitch running from the bark of the tree.

Mrs. B. gathered all of the children at the center of the tree farm for a meeting. She reminded the children of the importance of never giving up and said, "We just need to start over and we will succeed!" She began to speak to the children and to tell them, not to give up on the perfect tree.

The children all looked wide-eyed at Mrs. B. and nodded their heads up and down, as they believed they would find the perfect tree.

But, before they left the meeting, little Sara raised her hand, "Mrs. B., I am way shorter than all my friends in Pre-K. Am I imperfect?" And about that same time, Daniel's hand went up, and he asked, "Mrs. B, I am the tallest boy in my class, and sometimes, people call me 'stick boy', and 'giant boy'. Am I imperfect?"

And so it began. The hands began to rise and the questions of imperfection began by every boy and girl in the group that felt something about them was just not perfect. "I have brown eyes, and I wanted blue."

"I have red hair, and I wanted blonde."

"I can't run as fast as Caleb. Does that mean that I am not perfect?"

Affectionately, she looked at Danielle's blonde hair and said, "Blonde hair glistens in the sun, but so does Bobby's strawberry blonde and red highlights shine through Taryn's brown hair."

"I have freckles."

"I have two teeth missing."

All of the children began to point out their imagined flaws.

"I have this and I have that."

Mrs. B looked at Mrs. Bolden and then looked at the children.

As the hands began to go up in the air like kernels of corn popping, Mrs. B. cleared her throat and said, "Boys and girls, please put your hands down. I do believe I have made a mistake in telling you to look for perfection when what I should have said is find the one that you think is perfect and beautiful. Blue eyes are beautiful, but then again so are brown."

"The tree you choose may have a bare spot, a bushy top or an open spot in the middle. It may be tall. It may be short. But, if you think it is beautiful, then it is perfect!"

Once Mrs. B took the time to speak to the children and to answer their very important questions, the journey continued. They were determined to find the 'perfect tree' for Mrs. B.

When it was found, the children were content with their choice. It was perfectly imperfect!

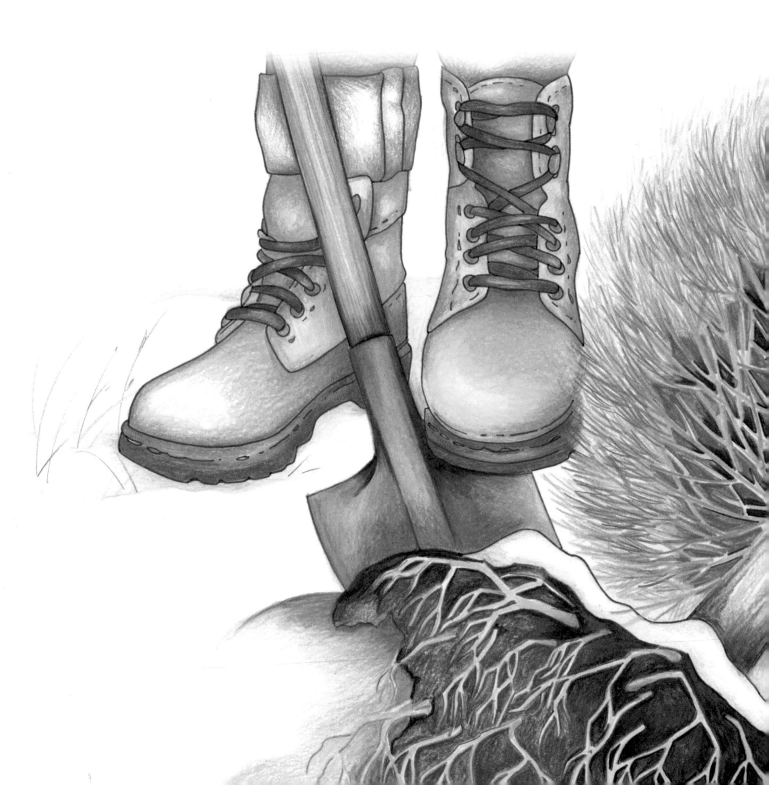

The tree was removed from the ground and placed in a big bucket of moist black soil. It was perfect for Mrs. B. and the children.

Mrs. B. loaded it in the pick-up and traveled to her home.

She beautifully decorated the tree and took several pictures of it to share with her students.

The children were most impressed with the tree. It was indeed the perfect tree for Mrs. B!

Printed in the United States
By Bookmasters